VINEGAR

VINEGAR

A BOOK OF RECIPES

HELEN SUDELL

LORENZ BOOKS

First published in 2015 by Lorenz Books
an imprint of Anness Publishing Limited
108 Great Russell Street, London WC1B 3NA
www.annesspublishing.com
info@anness.com
twitter: @Anness_Books

If you like the images in this book and would like to investigate using them for publishing, promotions or advertising, please visit our website www.practicalpictures.com for more information

A CIP catalogue record for this book is available from The British Library

Publisher Joanna Lorenz
Editorial Director Helen Sudell
Designer Nigel Partridge
Illustrations Anna Koska

Photographers: Martin Brigdale, Steve Moss, William Lingwood, Craig Robertson, Charlie Richards, Gus Filgate, Simon Smith, Debbie Patterson
Recipes by: Young Jin Song, Stuart Walton, Judith H. Dern, Janez Bogataj, Brian Glover, Ghillie Basan, Yasuko Fukuoka, Pepita Aris, Lucy Knox, Vilma Laus, Joanna Farrow, Alex Barker, Ann Nicol, Christine Ingram

Printed and bound in China

COOK'S NOTES

• Bracketed terms are intended for American readers.

• For all recipes, quantities are given in both metric and imperial measures and, where appropriate, in standard cups and spoons. Follow one set of measures, but not a mixture, because they are not interchangeable.

• Standard spoon and cup measures are level. 1 tsp = 5ml, 1 tbsp = 15ml, 1 cup = 250ml/8fl oz.

• Australian standard tablespoons are 20ml. Australian readers should use 3 tsp in place of 1 tbsp for measuring small quantities.

• American pints are 16fl oz/2 cups. American readers should use 20fl oz/2.5 cups in place of 1 pint when measuring liquids.

• Electric oven temperatures in this book are for conventional ovens. When using a fan oven, the temperature will probably need to be reduced by about 10–20°C/20–40°F. Since ovens vary, you should check with your manufacturer's instruction book for guidance.

• The nutritional analysis given for each recipe is calculated per portion (i.e. serving or item), unless otherwise stated. If the recipe gives a range, such as Serves 4–6, then the nutritional analysis will be for the smaller portion size, i.e. 6 servings. The analysis does not include optional ingredients, such as salt added to taste.

• Medium (US large) eggs are used unless otherwise stated.

PUBLISHER'S NOTE

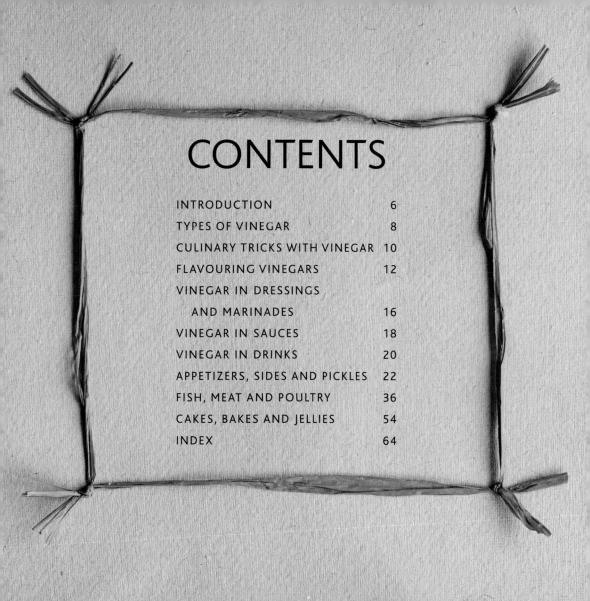

CONTENTS

INTRODUCTION

Vinegar is used for all sorts of cooking and while many methods are steeped in history, others are comparative newcomers to the culinary scene. Whether it is used for marinating, dressing, deglazing, sharpening, flavouring, or even raising cakes, the addition of vinegar will enrich and improve many dishes.

FOOD PREPARATION
Vinegar is used to rinse or soak food that naturally has an odour or for removing, or

Below: Add vinegar to water when washing salads to remove insects.

reducing, strong flavours that have developed when food has deteriorated slightly.

Vinegar can also be used to clean vegetables before cooking. Adding a little vinegar to a bowl of water in which fresh garden lettuce is washed brings out insects and bugs that otherwise manage to conceal themselves throughout several rinses. This method also works well for wild berries, such as raspberries, blackberries and blackcurrants, that tend to harbour tiny maggots.

Vinegar can be used to marinate savoury ingredients or macerate fruit. The choice of vinegar depends on the type of dish and whether it will be used in a sauce or discarded. Vinegar is also used in marinades to tenderize meat. It may be used with water or wine and the proportion is usually small. The majority of marinades and soaking mixtures are either used in the cooking liquid, to

Above: The acidity in balsamic vinegar enhances certain fruits.

baste food or served in a sauce. When macerating fruit, the vinegar usually acts as a dressing or sauce, or it is used as a syrup. Fine wine vinegars or fermented fruit vinegars are ideal for macerating fruit.

COOKING
One of the main contributions vinegar makes to food is to add a sharp flavour. When food is without any hint of acidity, a little vinegar accentuates the flavour and brings out the

characteristics of the ingredients, typically with fruit, such as blueberries, but also with vegetables, such as beetroot (beets). Flour-based sauces may be sharpened with a hint of vinegar or it can be used to bring contrast to soups and gravies.

Vinegar is excellent for balancing the richness of dishes and foods that have a high fat content. Examples include egg-based sauces and in roasting juices or sauces for rich and fatty foods, such as duck, pheasant or lamb.

Below: Vinegar is highly valued for its preservation properties.

PRESERVATION

The preservation properties of vinegar are fundamental to its culinary value, and it is for this purpose that vinegar is used in the largest proportion. It is present in a wide variety of preserves, with ingredients ranging from fish to fruit, and from simple pickles that require little preparation to more complex jellies and sauces.

FINISHING AND DRESSING

Added to a cooking pan after frying or roasting food, vinegar is used to loosen the residue and incorporate the juices and some fat in a sauce or gravy (this is called deglazing). Sauces made by deglazing have a more concentrated flavour, so a little is drizzled over each portion.

However, the simplest use of vinegar is as a straightforward dressing or condiment. It is drizzled over cooked or raw food or dishes to add piquancy and contrast. Partnered with oil (especially olive oil) it is used for a variety of dressings.

Above: Vinegar is often used with oil as a dressing.

VINEGAR DRESSING TIPS
When making a vinegar-based dressing always start with the vinegar, dissolving all the flavourings in it. Salt, sugar or mustard, for example, should be mixed into the vinegar first until dissolved (shaking in a screw-top jar will do the trick). Then add the virgin olive oil. This way the seasonings sing through the whole dressing rather than separating out as sediment at the bottom.

TYPES OF VINEGAR

From crystal-clear distilled malt vinegar to glossy, dark treacle-like balsamic, there is a vinegar to suit each food, every dish and all occasions.

BALSAMIC VINEGAR

Probably one of the most famous of vinegars, 'aceto balsamico' originates from northern Italy. The vinegar is fermented from a must of Trebbiano grapes. The cooked must is reduced to a dark syrup before it is ready for fermentation using a mother

preserved from previous batches. It is excellent on its own as a dip or condiment for bread, or as part of a rich dressing, sparingly drizzled over savoury or sweet dishes.

WINE VINEGAR

Different types of vinegar are made from wine.

Red or white vinegar is produced by fermenting wine, and varies in flavour and quality according to the type of wine, the fermentation process, and whether the vinegar has been matured. The majority of white wine vinegars are light and crisp, and some are very sharp. Red wine vinegars are pink to light red in colour and some are matured, with a stronger, fuller flavour.

They are used in hot and cold sauces, in salad dressings and as part of a marinade for fish.

Left: Balsamic vinegar is often used to deglaze pans.

Champagne vinegar is also known as Reims vinegar (vinaigre de Reims). It is aged in oak barrels for one year and is quite sharp but lighter in flavour than white or red wine vinegars. It is used in dressings, marinades and sauces or to sharpen drinks and desserts.

Sherry vinegar (vinagre de Jerez) is made in Spain and like other wine vinegars the quality and blend of sherries dictates the quality of the vinegar. Good sherry vinegar has its sharpness balanced by the full and distinct flavours of the original wine. The best can be mellow and rich, and compared by some to balsamic vinegar. It is often used in marinades for red meat, rich poultry and game. It also adds a hint of piquancy to rich gravies and sauces.

MALT VINEGAR

Rich, full-flavoured malted barley is fermented to produce alcohol and then onwards to make malt vinegar. Caramel is added to intensify the flavour and colour of the vinegar. Malt vinegar is famous as the condiment sprinkled on British fish and chips. It is also useful for pickling and making rich chutneys and ketchups.

Distilled malt vinegar, white vinegar or spirit vinegar is a concentrated malt vinegar with a higher acid content. This makes it ideal for preserving vegetables and other foods

Below: For pickling, malt vinegar is spiced with peppercorns, cloves and chillies.

with a high water content. **Light malt vinegar** is a pale gold-coloured vinegar brewed as for ordinary malt vinegar but without the addition of caramel. The flavour is milder and similar to rice vinegar.

Pickling vinegar is distilled malt vinegar flavoured with a mix of spices.

CIDER VINEGAR

Made from apples, apple juice or cider, this vinegar is milder than other wine and malt vinegars. Some are clear, others cloudy, and the colour varies from pale yellow to a honey-like gold. It has a reputation as a healing agent and general health-giving potion. Cider vinegar is said to make a positive contribution to everything from weight-loss and relieving arthritis to reducing cholesterol levels and the prevention of heart disease. In the kitchen, it brings piquancy to a wide variety of savoury or sweet dishes including cordials and sorbets.

Above: The finest cider vinegar is made from a single apple variety.

RICE VINEGAR

Fermented either from rice or from rice wine, rice vinegars vary in colour and flavour and have been an essential part of Asian cuisine for centuries. Available as white, red or black rice varieties, rice vinegar is prized for its health benefits, particularly in aiding digestion and easing some skin mild complaints.

In the kitchen it is used in meat dishes as a marinade and tenderizing agent, as a dipping sauce, and as a substitute for balsamic vinegar.

CULINARY TRICKS WITH VINEGAR

Vinegar is useful in the kitchen for improving the performance of ingredients or enhancing simple mixtures in a wide variety of ways.

POACHING EGGS

Adding vinegar to the poaching water makes the whites set more quickly.

Add 5ml/1 tsp vinegar to a pan of water and bring to the boil. Reduce to a simmer. Crack an egg into a cup, swirl the water with a spoon, then slip the egg into the middle of the swirl.

Poach the egg for 2–3 minutes in the simmering water. This will leave the yolk soft and runny. The circular swirl of water keeps the egg white in good shape, preventing it from spreading in strands, and the vinegar helps to set it.

Carefully remove the egg from the water using a slotted spoon and serve immediately.

PEELING EGGS

Adding a little vinegar to water makes it easier to peel hard-boiled eggs.

Add 5ml/1 tsp vinegar and 15ml/1 tbsp salt to boiling water before gently placing the eggs into the water.

MAKING EGGS GO FURTHER

This is an old-fashioned suggestion for making one egg do the work of two.

When baking a cake, use 15ml/1 tbsp vinegar with 1 egg instead of adding 2 eggs.

USING VINEGAR IN SWEET DISHES

Use sweetened fruit vinegars and balsamic vinegar to dress fruit for dessert. Serve alone or with whipped cream, fromage frais or yogurt.

Drizzle balsamic vinegar over pan-fried or grilled (broiled) fruit, such as bananas, peaches or pears. Serve fruit vinegars, such as raspberry or strawberry with plain vanilla mousse, cheesecake or ice cream for a tangy contrast.

STORING CHEESE

Wrapping cheese in a vinegar-soaked cloth before storing it in the refrigerator will keep it fresh and moist.

Place a little vinegar in a bowl. Soak a clean cloth or paper towel in the vinegar. Squeeze out most of the liquid, then use to wrap the cheese. Place in an airtight container and store in the refrigerator.

DESCALING FISH

Rubbing fish skin with vinegar will make it easier to remove the scales.

Place a little vinegar in a small bowl and rub it into the fish skin with your fingers.

Leave for 5 minutes, then descale the fish as usual. The vinegar will also help to reduce any fishy odour.

COOKING PASTA

Adding vinegar to the cooking water will prevent pasta from being sticky.

Bring a large pan of water to the boil. Instead of adding salt to the pan, add 5ml/1 tsp vinegar. Add the pasta and cook as usual. The addition of the vinegar will reduce the starch and make the pasta less sticky and easier to serve.

PRESERVING THE COLOUR OF VEGETABLES

Adding a little vinegar to the water will improve the colour of boiled vegetables.

Bring a large pan of water to the boil, then add 15ml/1 tbsp vinegar before carefully placing the vegetables in the water and cooking as usual. This will help them to retain their colour.

STORING VINEGAR

All varieties of vinegar should be stored in an airtight bottle in a cool, dark place. Those vinegars with live bacteria remaining will begin to ferment if not stored properly.

Distilled vinegars will keep indefinitely, although the flavour will lose strength. However, it is a good idea to use all vinegar by the date suggested on the label. If vinegar smells bad, it should be discarded.

FLAVOURING VINEGARS

A wide variety of commercially produced flavoured vinegars are available, but it is easy and fun to try making your own.

There are endless possibilities for flavouring vinegars at home, from spicing inexpensive vinegar for pickling to flower-scented vinegars and vibrant fruit vinegars.

Experiment with fresh garden produce, lively herbs and favourite spices to make a range of vinegars that can be used to infuse exciting flavours into salad dressings and sauces.

The choice of vinegar depends on its likely uses. Malt is ideal for pickles and chutneys. Wine vinegar will go well in some dressings or for deglazing a cooking pan but may be too harsh for dressing a fruit dessert.

Cider vinegar will be useful for dressings, sauces and drinks. Experiment with different vinegars until you find the one you prefer.

CHILLI VINEGAR

Easy to make with dried or fresh chillies, this chilli vinegar can be added to many dishes to give them that extra bite.

Pour a little white wine vinegar out of the bottle and reserve. Place 1–2 dried red chillies or 1–3 fresh green chillies in the bottle then refill with the white wine vinegar. Seal. Leave the chilli vinegar to infuse in a cool, dark place for anything from a week to 6 months.

GINGER VINEGAR

Use spicy vinegar in oriental cooking, in stir-fried dishes or dipping sauces.

Finely chop a piece of fresh root ginger, about 4cm/1½in. Simmer the ginger in 5cm/2in vinegar in a covered pan for 30 minutes. Cool before transferring to a sterilized glass container, then pour on enough vinegar to fill. Seal and infuse for 1 month. Strain and add sugar to taste before bottling.

GARLIC VINEGAR

Use this to make delicious marinades for fish, shellfish and chicken.

Peel and halve 1 large or 2 small cloves of garlic, then add the garlic to a bottle of vinegar. Seal, and leave to stand for at least a week, then strain and bottle the vinegar.

CELERY VINEGAR

This can be added to soups, sauces or salad dressings.

Slice 1–2 celery stalks lengthways. Place the celery in a jar, without packing in tightly. Pour in vinegar to cover, shaking out all the air, cover

HERB AND FLOWER VINEGARS

White wine or cider vinegar is best for making flower or herb vinegars. Herb and flower vinegars should be strained, but you can add a few fresh sprigs of herb when bottling to indicate the flavour. Make sure that flowers are edible before putting them to food use in vinegars. Common edible flowers include nasturtium, rose, pansy, citrus blossom, lilac, violet and honeysuckle.

and leave to stand for 3–4 weeks. Strain and bottle the vinegar in a sterilized container.

TARRAGON VINEGAR

A wide variety of herbs can be used to flavour vinegar, either individually or mixed. Tarragon vinegar is a classic ingredient for salad dressings and egg sauces.

Wash and dry 15g/½oz/¾ cup fresh tarragon and remove the leaves from the stalks. Place in a container and pour on 450ml/¾ pint/scant 2 cups white wine vinegar. Seal and leave to stand for 4 weeks in a cool, dark place. Strain and bottle in a sterilized container.

NASTURTIUM FLOWER VINEGAR

Serve this as a dressing for salads containing nasturtium flowers.

Place a handful of nasturtium flowers in a jar, filling it without squashing the flowers. Pour in wine vinegar to cover, gently agitate the jar to remove trapped air, and cover. Leave to mature for 2 months. Strain the vinegar through muslin or cheesecloth, squeezing out all the vinegar from the flowers.

ROSE PETAL VINEGAR

For a refreshingly and prettily coloured dressing make this with Champagne vinegar.

Pull the rose petals from 2 or 3 scented rose heads. Snip off the bitter white heel at the base of each petal. Place 2 handfuls of petals in a large glass jar or bottle. Fill the jar or bottle with Champagne or white wine vinegar, seal very tightly with a screw-top or cork and leave on a sunny windowsill for at least 3 weeks before straining.

FRUIT-FLAVOURED VINEGARS

White vinegar can be used for preparing large quantities but cider and wine vinegars can give better flavours and are practical for making smaller quantities. The washed fruit should be left to stand in the vinegar for 5–7 days before straining. When making small quantities to be used relatively quickly, there is no need to heat the vinegar. When preparing a large volume for long-term storage, the vinegar should be boiled before storing otherwise it will ferment with time.

RASPBERRY VINEGAR

One of the classics, this is simple to make with fresh or frozen raspberries. There is little point in buying raspberry flavoured vinegar when it can be made so easily at home using a favourite wine or cider vinegar and just the right hint of sweetness.

Macerate 450g/1lb raspberries, fresh or frozen raspberries in 1.2 litres/2 pints/5 cups vinegar for about 5 days. Strain through a sieve or strainer lined with muslin or cheesecloth. Heat with 450g/1lb sugar until dissolved, then bring to the boil. Bottle, cover immediately and cool.

RICH BLACKBERRY VINEGAR

Mixed with sparkling water and a sprig of mint, this makes a refreshing drink.

Measure a jug or pitcher of blackberries and add the same volume of vinegar. Cover and stand for 1 day. Strain, add another jug of berries, cover and leave for a further day. Strain and repeat again. Strain and add 450g/1lb sugar for every 600ml/1 pint/2½ cups vinegar. Heat until dissolved, then bring to the boil. Reduce the heat and simmer for 30 minutes. Bottle and mature for 4 weeks before using.

CITRUS VINEGAR

This makes a great marinade ingredient for fish dishes.

Pare off the thin outer rind of 1 orange, lemon or lime using a vegetable peeler. Also remove all the bitter white pith. Place a few strips of the peel in a bottle of vinegar and allow to infuse for 3–6 weeks. Using a mixture of different coloured fruits will give an attractive result. Alternatively, add the grated zest of 1 lemon, lime or orange to a bottle of vinegar.

VINEGAR IN DRESSINGS AND MARINADES

Vinegar is an essential ingredient in many dressings and marinades, whether you wish to add an edge to creamy dressings or a sharpness to herbs and oils.

CLASSIC VINAIGRETTE
Make sure all the ingredients are at room temperature to make a smooth emulsion.

Put 30ml/2 tbsp balsamic vinegar in a bowl with 10ml/ 2 tsp Dijon mustard, salt and ground black pepper. Whisk to combine. Drizzle in 90ml/6 tbsp olive oil, whisking until the vinaigrette is well blended.

HAZELNUT DRESSING
Serve this with a goat's cheese salad and chopped hazelnuts.

Put 30ml/2 tbsp hazelnut oil in a small bowl. Add 5–10ml/ 1–2 tsp sherry vinegar to taste, and whisk the oil and vinegar together thoroughly. Season to taste with salt and ground black pepper.

DILL DRESSING
Serve this simple mixture of oil, vinegar and dill with smoked fish.

Whisk 90ml/6 tbsp olive oil and 30ml/2 tbsp white wine

vinegar together, or shake in a screw-top jar. Blend in 15ml/ 1 tbsp chopped fresh dill and season to taste.

GARLIC RASPBERRY DRESSING
Adding a splash of raspberry vinegar to this dressing enlivens a simple salad.

Fry 2 finely sliced garlic cloves in 45ml/3 tbsp olive oil until just golden. Remove with a slotted spoon and drain on kitchen paper. Pour the oil into a bowl and whisk in the raspberry vinegar. Season with salt and ground black pepper.

HOISIN MARINADE
Use this Chinese marinade for chops and chicken pieces.

Combine 175ml/6fl oz/1 cup hoisin sauce, 30ml/2 tbsp each sesame oil, dry sherry and rice vinegar, 4 chopped garlic cloves, 2.5ml/½ tsp soft light brown sugar and 1.5ml/¼ tsp five-spice powder.

TERIYAKI MARINADE
Soy sauce is paired with rice vinegar in this Japanese recipe.

In a bowl, combine 1 crushed garlic clove, 5ml/1 tsp grated fresh root ginger, 30ml/2 tbsp soy sauce and 15ml/1 tbsp rice vinegar.

SHERRY VINEGAR MARINADE
This piquant mix would suit fish or meat.

In a bowl, combine 30ml/ 2 tbsp sherry vinegar with 45ml/3 tbsp garlic-infused oil and season to taste.

SUMMER HERB MARINADE
Raid the herb garden to make this fresh-tasting marinade, which can be used to enliven prepared vegetables, poultry and meat ready for grilling on the barbecue.

In a bowl, combine 45ml/ 3 tbsp tarragon vinegar (see page 13), 1 crushed garlic clove and 2 finely chopped spring onions (scallions). Whisk in 90ml/6 tbsp olive oil, then add a large handful of chopped fresh herbs such as thyme, flat leaf parsley and basil and mix well. Season with salt and ground black pepper.

VINEGAR IN SAUCES

Vinegar serves a sharpening and/or mixing function to add piquancy or bring flavours together effectively in many classic sauces.

TARTARE SAUCE

This creamy sauce is the traditional accompaniment to fish dishes.

Makes 475ml/16fl oz/2 cups

1 egg yolk
15ml/1 tbsp white wine vinegar
30ml/2 tbsp Dijon-style mustard
250ml/8 fl oz/1 cup groundnut (peanut) oil
30ml/2 tbsp fresh lemon juice
45ml/3 tbsp finely chopped spring onions (scallions)
30ml/2 tbsp chopped capers
45ml/3 tbsp finely chopped sour dill pickles
45ml/3 tbsp finely chopped fresh parsley

In a bowl, beat the egg yolk with a wire whisk. Add the white wine vinegar and

mustard and continue to whisk for about 10 seconds. Whisk the oil into the mixture in a slow, steady stream.

Add the lemon juice, spring onions, capers, sour dill pickles and parsley and mix well. Keep chilled; use within 2 days.

MINT SAUCE

This sauce is classically served with roast lamb.

Makes 300ml/½ pint/ 1¼ cups

1 large bunch mint
105ml/7 tbsp boiling water
150ml/¼ pint/⅔ cup wine vinegar
30ml/2 tbsp sugar

Finely chop the mint and place in a 600ml/1-pint/2¼-cup jug or pitcher.

Pour the boiling water slowly into the jug, covering the mint, and then leave it to infuse for about 10 minutes.

When the mint infusion has cooled until it has reached a lukewarm temperature, stir in the wine vinegar and sugar.

Continue stirring (but do not mash up). Mint sauce will keep for up to 6 months stored in the refrigerator, but it is best used within 3 weeks.

HORSERADISH SAUCE

This has a very strong flavour that complements steak or roast beef.

**Makes about 200ml/
7fl oz/scant 1 cup**
45ml/3 tbsp horseradish root
15ml/1 tbsp white wine vinegar
5ml/1 tsp sugar
pinch of salt
*150ml/¼ pint/²⁄₃ cup thick
    double (heavy) cream, for
    serving*

Peel the horseradish root and grate it finely in a food processor. Horseradish is

powerful, so submerge it in water while you peel it. Place the grated horseradish in a bowl, then wash your hands.

Add the white wine vinegar to the bowl, with the sugar and the salt. Stir until thoroughly combined.

Pour into a sterilized jar. It will keep in the refrigerator for 6 months. A few hours before serving the sauce, stir in the cream.

HOLLANDAISE SAUCE

This is an essential part of Eggs Benedict, but is also delicious served on vegetables.

**Makes about 135ml/4fl oz/
½ cup**
*115g/4oz/½ cup unsalted
    butter*
2 egg yolks
*15–30ml/1–2 tbsp white wine
    vinegar or tarragon vinegar*
salt and ground white pepper

Melt the butter in a small pan over a medium heat. Put the egg yolks and vinegar in a small

bowl. Add salt and pepper and whisk until the mixture is completely smooth.

Slowly pour the melted butter in a steady stream on to the egg yolk mixture, beating vigorously the whole time with a wooden spoon to make a smooth, creamy sauce.

Taste the sauce and add more vinegar, and season, if necessary. Serve.

COOK'S TIP

Instead of adding the butter to the egg mixture in the bowl, you could put the mixture in a food processor and add the butter through the feeder tube, with the motor running.

VINEGAR IN DRINKS

A little vinegar in sparkling mineral water makes a refreshing drink and an excellent alternative to an alcoholic cocktail or glass of wine. It is also used to give an edge to some cocktails.

VIRGIN PRAIRIE OYSTER

This delicious non-alcoholic version of the classic hangover cure will help you to avoid the headache altogether.

Makes one tall glass
*175ml/6fl/³⁄₄ cup tomato
   juice
10ml/2 tsp Worcestershire
   sauce
5–10ml/1–2 tsp balsamic
   vinegar
1 egg yolk
cayenne pepper, to taste*

Measure the tomato juice into a large glass and pour over plenty of ice until well chilled.
   Strain into a tall tumbler half-filled with ice cubes.

Add the Worcestershire sauce and balsamic vinegar to taste and mix with a swizzle-stick.
   Carefully float the egg yolk on top of the drink and lightly dust with cayenne pepper.

PRAIRIE OYSTER

This cocktail, containing a dash of white wine vinegar, is said to cure hangovers.

Makes one shot
*20ml/1½ tbsp sweet Madeira,
   or cognac
10ml/2 tsp white wine vinegar*

*5ml/1 tsp Worcestershire sauce
pinch cayenne pepper
dash Tabasco
1 egg yolk*

Add the Madeira or cognac, white wine vinegar, Worcestershire sauce, cayenne pepper and Tabasco to a small tumbler.
   Mix well without ice, and then spoon the yolk very gently on top.
   The preparation should then be swallowed in one gulp, without breaking the egg yolk.

SPARKLING ELDERFLOWER DRINK

This is a delightful, sparkling and refreshing non-alcoholic drink that is easy to make. It will keep in airtight bottles for up to a month.

Makes 9 litres/2 gallons/ 2.4 US gallons

24 elderflower heads
2 lemons
1.3kg/3lb/scant 7 cups granulated (white) sugar
30ml/2 tbsp white wine vinegar
9 litres/2 gallons/2.4 US gallons water

Find a clean bucket that you can cover with a clean cloth. Put all the ingredients into it. Cover the bucket with a plastic sheet and leave overnight.

Strain the elderflower drink then pour into bottles, leaving a space of about 2.5cm/1in at the top.

Seal the bottles and leave for 2 weeks in a cool place, for fermentation to take place. Serve chilled.

VINEGAR SPRITZERS

Mixing a little vinegar with mineral water makes a surprisingly tasty summer drink.

Makes one glass

10ml/2 tsp fruit vinegar, such as raspberry, fig or blackberry
slices of cucumber, orange and apple
sprig of fresh mint
sparkling mineral water

Pour the fruit vinegar into a glass. Add the slices of cucumber, orange and apple with a sprig of fresh mint and top up with sparkling water.

VINEGAR SMOOTHIES

Adding vinegar to fresh fruit smoothies gives them a tangy kick.

Makes one large glass

300ml/½ pint/1¼ cup natural (plain) yogurt
15ml/1 tbsp fruit vinegar, such as raspberry, orange or blackberry
fresh fruit juice, such as apple, pineapple or grape

Pour the yogurt into a tall glass and add the fruit vinegar.

Top up the glass with fruit juice and serve.

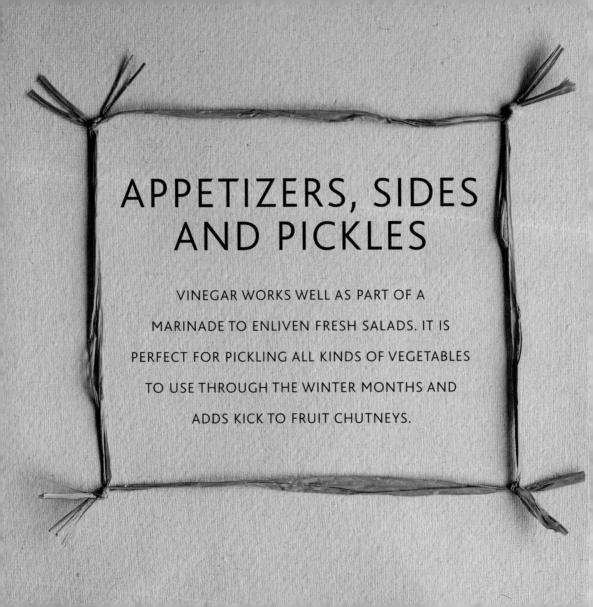

APPETIZERS, SIDES AND PICKLES

VINEGAR WORKS WELL AS PART OF A
MARINADE TO ENLIVEN FRESH SALADS. IT IS
PERFECT FOR PICKLING ALL KINDS OF VEGETABLES
TO USE THROUGH THE WINTER MONTHS AND
ADDS KICK TO FRUIT CHUTNEYS.

ANCHOVY AND ROASTED PEPPER SALAD

The rich balsamic vinegar in this salad really brings out the flavour of the roasted peppers.
This salad will keep refrigerated for up to two days.

Serves 4

2 red, 2 orange and 2 yellow
    (bell) peppers, halved and
    seeded
50g/2oz can anchovies in
    olive oil
2 garlic cloves
45ml/3 tbsp balsamic vinegar
salt and ground black pepper

Energy 108kcal/453kJ; Protein 6g;
Carbohydrate 16.4g, of which sugars 15.5g;
Fat 2.4g, of which saturates 0.5g;
Cholesterol 8mg; Calcium 83mg; Fibre
4.6g; Sodium 506mg.

Preheat the oven to 200°C/400°F/Gas 6. Place the peppers, cut side down, in a roasting pan. Roast for 40 minutes, until the skins are charred. Transfer the peppers to a bowl, cover with clear film (plastic wrap) and leave for 15 minutes.

Peel the peppers, then cut them into chunky strips. Drain the anchovies, reserving the olive oil, and halve the fillets lengthways.

Slice the garlic as thinly as possible and place it in a large bowl. Stir in the olive oil, vinegar and a little pepper. Add the peppers and anchovies and use a spoon and fork to fold the ingredients together. Cover and chill until ready to serve.

VINEGARED CUCUMBER SALAD

This light, refreshing salad is served with all kinds of poached fish. The vinegar and sugar dressing should be perfectly balanced between sweet and sour, with accents of fresh dill.

Serves 6

1 large English cucumber, about 35cm/14in long
75ml/5 tbsp distilled white vinegar
25g/1oz/2 tbsp white sugar
45ml/3 tbsp chopped fresh dill
salt and ground white pepper

COOK'S TIP
The vinegar and sugar can also be mixed into 250ml/8fl oz/1 cup sour cream for a richer, cream-style dressing that goes well with fish cakes and fried fish.

Energy 30kcal/125kJ; Protein 0.7g; Carbohydrate 1.1g, of which sugars 1g; Fat 2.6g, of which saturates 1.6g; Cholesterol 8mg; Calcium 26mg; Fibre 0.4g; Sodium 8mg.

Cut the cucumber into 3mm/⅛in slices and place in a serving bowl.
Combine the vinegar, sugar and dill in a small bowl and season with salt and pepper. Pour the dressing over the cucumber slices and toss to coat evenly. Chill until ready to serve.

SAUERKRAUT SALAD IN VINEGAR

Made with a combination of raw and cooked diced vegetables, the salad is mixed with sauerkraut and is an excellent accompaniment to omelettes, sliced cold meats, or sausages.

Serves 4

450g/1lb sauerkraut
115g/4oz/1 cup diced cooked beetroot (beets)
2 large carrots, peeled and coarsely grated
115g/4oz/1 cup diced cucumber
50g/2oz/½ cup diced celery
225g/8oz/2 cups diced cooked potatoes
6 gherkins, very finely chopped
60ml/4 tbsp chopped fresh parsley
75ml/2½fl oz/⅓ cup light olive or vegetable oil
30ml/2 tbsp cider vinegar
5ml/1 tsp wholegrain mustard
salt and ground black pepper

Drain the sauerkraut in a sieve or strainer, then roughly chop it into smaller pieces. Put it in a bowl with all the grated and diced beetroot, carrots, cucumber, celery and potatoes, along with half of the chopped gherkins and half of the parsley. Gently mix together.

Whisk the oil, vinegar, mustard, salt and pepper together in a small jug, pitcher or bowl with a fork, or shake together well in a screw-top jar. Drizzle the mixture over the vegetables and mix well.

Transfer the salad to a serving bowl or platter and serve sprinkled with the remaining gherkins and parsley.

Energy 204kcal/844kJ; Protein 4.2g;
Carbohydrate 17.4g, of which sugars 8.6g;
Fat 13.4g, of which saturates 1.9g;
Cholesterol 0mg; Calcium 122mg; Fibre
5.7g; Sodium 823mg.

GAZPACHO

This classic Spanish chilled soup is deeply rooted in the province of Andalusia. The sherry vinegar adds a sweet richness to the tomato and pepper sauce.

Serves 4

1.3–1.6kg/3–3½lb ripe
   tomatoes
1 green (bell) pepper, seeded
   and roughly chopped
2 garlic cloves, finely chopped
2 slices stale bread, crusts
   removed
60ml/4 tbsp extra virgin olive oil
60ml/4 tbsp sherry vinegar
150ml/¼ pint/⅔ cup tomato
   juice
300ml/½ pint/1¼ cups iced
   water
salt and ground black pepper
ice cubes, to serve (optional)

For the garnishes

30ml/2 tbsp olive oil
2–3 slices stale bread, diced
1 small cucumber, peeled
   and finely diced
1 small onion, finely chopped
1 red (bell) and 1 green (bell)
   pepper, seeded and finely
   diced
2 hard-boiled eggs, chopped

Skin the tomatoes, then quarter them and remove the cores and seeds, saving the juices. Put the pepper in a food processor and process for a few seconds. Add the tomatoes, reserved juices, garlic, bread, oil and vinegar and process. Add the tomato juice and blend to combine.

Season the soup, then pour into a large bowl, cover with clear film (plastic wrap) and chill for at least 12 hours.

Prepare the garnishes. Heat the olive oil in a frying pan and fry the bread cubes for 4–5 minutes until golden brown and crisp. Drain well on kitchen paper, then arrange in a small dish. Place each of the remaining garnishes in separate small dishes.

Just before serving, dilute the soup with the ice-cold water. The consistency should be thick but not too stodgy. If you like, stir a few ice cubes into the soup, then spoon into serving bowls and serve with the prepared garnishes.

Energy 376kcal/1584kJ; Protein 11.3g; Carbohydrate 38.3g, of which sugars 31.3g; Fat 21.1g, of which saturates 3.6g; Cholesterol 95mg; Calcium 109mg; Fibre 8.3g; Sodium 1032mg.

PICKLED BEETROOT

Dark purple beetroot are highly nutritious and easy to preserve. Try pickling them in vinegar for use in salads and soups, to serve as side dishes and to garnish open sandwiches.

Serves 6

1.2kg/2½lb fresh beetroot (beets), preferably with stems attached
45ml/3 tbsp distilled white vinegar

For the marinade

120ml/4fl oz/½ cup water
60ml/4 tbsp distilled white vinegar
90g/3½oz/½ cup sugar
1 bay leaf
2.5ml/½ tsp caraway seeds
3 whole cloves
salt and ground black pepper

Energy 115kcal/490kJ; Protein 2.7g; Carbohydrate 27.4g, of which sugars 26.5g; Fat 0.2g, of which saturates 0g; Cholesterol 0mg; Calcium 39mg; Fibre 2.9g; Sodium 430mg.

Trim the beetroot stems to 2.5cm/1in, but do not peel the skins or cut the roots. Place 2 litres/3½ pints water and the vinegar in a deep pan and bring to the boil. Add the beetroot, adding more water if necessary to cover them, and simmer for about 45 minutes until tender. Remove from the heat, drain the beetroot, reserving 250ml/8fl oz/1 cup of the cooking liquid, and allow them to cool.

To prepare the marinade, combine all the ingredients in a pan and bring to the boil. Remove from the heat, pour into a large bowl and leave until cool.

Peel the cooled beetroot and cut them into 5mm/¼in slices. Add the slices to the bowl with the marinade and toss gently to coat. Cover the bowl and refrigerate for 8 hours or overnight.

BRAISED RED CABBAGE

Sweet, tangy red cabbage, simmered gently in vinegar and water, is a wintertime favourite.
Outstanding paired with roast pork it also goes well with roast turkey or duck.

Serves 6

1.3kg/3lb red cabbage
50ml/2fl oz/¼ cup distilled
*   white vinegar*
25g/1oz/2 tbsp butter
1 medium onion, finely chopped
2 tart apples, peeled, cored and
*   thinly sliced*
50g/2oz/¼ cup sugar
120ml/4fl oz/½ cup
*   blackcurrant juice or jam*
1.5ml/¼ tsp ground allspice
6 whole cloves
salt

> **COOK'S TIP**
> Substitute the blackcurrant
> juice or jam with apple
> redcurrant jelly or apple
> juice, if you prefer.

Energy 90kcal/381kJ; Protein 3.1g;
Carbohydrate 19.4g, of which sugars 18g;
Fat 0.5g, of which saturates 0g; Cholesterol
0mg; Calcium 98mg; Fibre 5g; Sodium
14mg.

Remove the outer leaves and core of the cabbage and cut into quarters.
Thinly chop or shred the cabbage, and place in a large pan. Add 120ml/
4fl oz/½ cup water and the vinegar and bring to the boil. Reduce the
heat, cover and simmer for 1 hour, stirring occasionally to prevent
scorching.

Meanwhile, melt the butter in a large frying pan over a medium heat.
Stir in the onion and apples and cook for 5–7 minutes until soft.

Stir the cooked apples and onion into the cabbage with the sugar,
blackcurrant juice or jam, allspice and cloves, and season with salt.
Simmer gently for a further 1½ hours. Adjust the seasoning to taste
before serving.

PICKLED ONIONS

These powerful pickles should be made with malt vinegar and stored for at least 6 weeks before eating. They can be enjoyed with cold meats or a mature hard cheese and crusty bread.

Makes 1.8kg/4 lb

1kg/2¼lb pickling onions, peeled
115g/4oz/½ cup salt
750ml/1¼ pints/3 cups malt vinegar
15ml/1 tbsp sugar
2–3 dried red chillies
5ml/1 tsp brown mustard seeds
15ml/1 tbsp coriander seeds
5ml/1 tsp allspice berries
5ml/1 tsp black peppercorns
5cm/2in piece fresh root ginger, sliced
2–3 blades mace
2–3 fresh bay leaves

Energy 669kcal/2,775kJ; Protein 48.7g; Carbohydrate 5g, of which sugars 3.8g; Fat 45.9g, of which saturates 11.1g; Cholesterol 250mg; Calcium 37mg; Fibre 0.9g; Sodium 196mg.

Place the peeled onions in a bowl, cover with cold water, then drain the water into a pan. Add the salt and heat slightly to dissolve, then cool before pouring the brine over the onions.

Place a plate inside the top of the bowl and weigh it down to keep all the onions submerged in the brine. Leave to stand for 24 hours.

Meanwhile, place the vinegar in a large pan. Wrap all the remaining ingredients, except the bay leaves, in a piece of muslin or cheesecloth. Bring to the boil, simmer for about 5 minutes, then remove the pan from the heat. Set aside and leave to infuse overnight.

The next day, drain the onions, rinse and pat dry. Pack them into sterilized 450g/1lb jars. Add the spices from the vinegar, except the ginger. Pour the vinegar over to cover and add the bay leaves.

Seal the jars with non-metallic lids and store in a cool, dark place.

PICKLED GINGER

Warming, good for the heart, and believed to aid digestion, ginger finds its way into oriental cooking in many dishes. Pickled in rice vinegar it is often served as a condiment with broths, noodles and rice.

Serves 4–6

225g/8oz fresh young ginger, peeled
10ml/2 tsp salt
200ml/7fl oz/1 cup white rice vinegar
50g/2oz/¼ cup sugar

Place the ginger in a bowl and sprinkle with salt. Cover and place in the refrigerator for at least 24 hours.

Drain off any excess liquid and pat the ginger dry with a clean dish towel. Slice each knob of ginger very finely along the grain, like thin rose petals, and place them in a clean bowl or a sterilized jar suitable for storing.

In a small bowl, beat the vinegar and 50ml/2fl oz/¼ cup cold water with the sugar, until it has all completely dissolved.

Pour the pickling liquid over the ginger and cover or seal. Store in the refrigerator or a cool place for about 1 week.

Energy 36kcal/151kJ; Protein 0.2g; Carbohydrate 9.1g, of which sugars 9.1g; Fat 0.1g, of which saturates 0g; Cholesterol 0mg; Calcium 20mg; Fibre 0.4g; Sodium 678mg.

TART TOMATO RELISH

Adding lime and white wine vinegar to this relish gives it a wonderfully tangy flavour. Perfect for coping with a glut of summer tomatoes, it makes a great dish to accompany tortilla chips.

Makes about 500g/1¼lb

2 pieces preserved stem ginger
1 lime
450g/1lb cherry tomatoes
115g/4oz/½ cup muscovado (molasses) sugar
120ml/4fl oz/½ cup white wine vinegar
5ml/1 tsp salt

Coarsely chop the preserved stem ginger. Slice the lime thinly, including the rind, then chop into small pieces. Place the cherry tomatoes, sugar, vinegar, salt, ginger and lime in a large heavy pan.

Bring to the boil, stirring until the sugar dissolves. Simmer rapidly for 45 minutes. Stir until the liquid has evaporated and the relish is thick and pulpy.

Leave to cool for about 5 minutes, then spoon into sterilized jars. Leave to cool, then cover and store in the refrigerator for up to 1 month.

Energy 530kcal/2262kJ; Protein 3.7g; Carbohydrate 134.1g, of which sugars 134.1g; Fat 1.4g, of which saturates 0.5g; Cholesterol 0mg; Calcium 93mg; Fibre 4.5g; Sodium 2012mg.

KASHMIR CHUTNEY

This sweet, chunky, spicy chutney is perfect served with cold meats. The sweetness of the apples and raisins is perfectly offset by the spicy ginger and warming malt vinegar.

Makes about 2.75kg/6lb

1kg/2¼lb green eating apples
15g/½oz garlic cloves
1 litre/1¾ pints/4 cups malt vinegar
450g/1lb dates
115g/4oz preserved stem ginger
450g/1lb/3 cups raisins
450g/1lb/2 cups soft light brown sugar
2.5ml/½ tsp cayenne pepper
30ml/2 tbsp salt

Energy 3920kcal/16,737kJ; Protein 22.6g; Carbohydrate 1014.4g, of which sugars 1012.2g; Fat 3.3g, of which saturates 0g; Cholesterol 0mg; Calcium 599mg; Fibre 33.7g; Sodium 12139mg.

Quarter the apples, remove the cores and chop coarsely. Peel and chop the garlic.

Place the apple with the chopped garlic in a pan with enough vinegar to cover. Bring to the boil and boil for 10 minutes.

Chop the dates and ginger and add them to the pan, with the rest of the ingredients. Cook gently for 45 minutes.

Spoon the mixture into warmed sterilized jars and seal immediately.

Store in a cool, dark place and use within 1 year. Once opened, store in the refrigerator and use within 2 months.

CHUNKY PEAR AND WALNUT CHUTNEY

The perfect balance of cider vinegar and tart apples and pears makes this a surprisingly mellow accompaniment to cheese as well as grains, including pilaffs and tabbouleh.

Makes about 1.8kg/4lb

1.2kg/2½lb firm pears
225g/8oz tart cooking apples
225g/8oz onions
450ml/¾ pint/scant 2 cups cider vinegar
175g/6oz/generous 1 cup sultanas (golden raisins)
finely grated rind and juice of 1 orange
400g/14oz/2 cups sugar
115g/4oz/1 cup walnuts, roughly chopped
2.5ml/½ tsp ground cinnamon

COOK'S TIP

To sterilize storage jars, place them in a dishwasher on a hot setting.

Alternatively, wash and dry them and place upside down in an oven 110°C/ 225°F/Gas ¼ and bake for 30 minutes. Allow to cool slightly before filling.

Peel and core the pears and apples, then chop them into 2.5cm/1in chunks. Peel and quarter the onions, then chop into pieces of about the same size.

Place in a preserving pan with the vinegar. Slowly bring to the boil, then reduce the heat and simmer for 40 minutes, until the apples, pears and onions are tender, stirring occasionally.

Meanwhile, put the sultanas in a bowl, pour over the orange juice and leave to soak.

Add the sugar, sultanas, and orange rind and juice to the pan.

Gently heat the mixture until the sugar has dissolved, then simmer for 30–40 minutes, or until the chutney is thick and no excess liquid remains. Stir frequently towards the end of cooking to prevent the chutney sticking on the bottom of the pan.

Gently toast the walnuts in a non-stick pan over a low heat, stirring constantly, for 5 minutes, until golden. Stir the nuts into the chutney with the cinnamon.

Spoon the chutney into warmed sterilized jars, cover and seal. Store in a cool, dark place, then leave to mature for at least 1 month. Use within 1 year. Once opened, store in the refrigerator and use within 2 months.

Energy 3501kcal/14,797kJ; Protein 29.8g; Carbohydrate 705.3g, of which sugars 699.3g; Fat 81.4g, of which saturates 6.4g; Cholesterol 0mg; Calcium 603mg; Fibre 40.7g; Sodium 189mg.

FISH, MEAT
AND POULTRY

WHETHER AS PART OF A MARINADE TO CUT
THROUGH RICH, OILY FISH, INCLUDED IN A SPICY
SAUCE TO ACCOMPANY POULTRY, OR AS A SWEET
TOMATO SALSA TO SERVE WITH STEAK, VINEGAR
ADDS PUNGENCY TO ALL KINDS OF MAIN MEALS.

JAPANESE CRAB MEAT IN VINEGAR

Delicately flavoured rice vinegar is used widely in Japanese cooking – here it is simply combined with a little sugar and soy sauce to produce a tasty dressing for crab.

Serves 4

½ red (bell) pepper, seeded and
   sliced
pinch of salt
275g/10oz cooked white crab
   meat
about 300g/11oz cucumber,
   seeds removed

For the vinegar mixture

15ml/1 tbsp rice vinegar
10ml/2 tsp caster (superfine)
   sugar
10ml/2 tsp shoyu (soy sauce)

Energy 82kcal/345kJ; Protein 13.3g;
Carbohydrate 5.6g, of which sugars 5.4g;
Fat 0.8g, of which saturates 0.1g;
Cholesterol 50mg; Calcium 100mg; Fibre
0.9g; Sodium 560mg.

Sprinkle the pepper slices with salt and leave for 15 minutes. Rinse well and drain.

Combine the rice vinegar, sugar and shoyu in a bowl.

Loosen the crab meat and mix it with the pepper. Divide among four bowls.

Finely grate the cucumber. Mix the grated cucumber with the vinegar mixture, and pour a quarter into each bowl. Serve immediately.

TUNA IN THE STYLE OF ALGHERO

This Italian dish is a really unusual way of cooking a tuna loin, which is soaked in water and white wine vinegar then baked and served thickly sliced. The soaking keeps it extra moist.

Serves 4–6

1kg/2¼lb fresh tuna loin
100ml/3½fl oz/scant ½ cup
white wine vinegar
100ml/3½fl oz/scant ½ cup
extra virgin olive oil
1 onion, finely chopped
1 small celery stick, finely
chopped
3 dried bay leaves
200ml/7fl oz/scant 1 cup dry
white wine
30g/1¼oz/generous ¼ cup
pitted black olives
sea salt

Put the tuna into a large, deep bowl of cold water and add the vinegar. Leave to soak for 2 hours. Drain and pat dry on kitchen paper.

Heat the oil in a large, heavy frying pan, add the onion, celery and bay leaves, and fry gently for 5–10 minutes, until the onion is soft.

Add the tuna loin to the pan and cook gently, turning frequently, for 20 minutes.

Add the white wine to the pan and cook for 1–2 minutes to allow the alcohol to evaporate.

Add the olives and season with salt, then cover and simmer over a low heat for a further 10 minutes.

Thickly slice the tuna loin, then serve it on a warmed platter, with the sauce from the pan drizzled over.

Energy 365kcal/1526kJ; Protein 40g; Carbohydrate 2.9g, of which sugars 2.1g; Fat 19.3g, of which saturates 3.6g; Cholesterol 47mg; Calcium 43mg; Fibre 0.7g; Sodium 196mg.

FISH IN CARPIONE

Carpione is an Italian cooking term meaning marinated in herbs and vinegar. This cold recipe uses sea fish fillets that are cooked and then left to marinate overnight. Start preparations the day before.

Serves 8

plain (all-purpose) flour, for
*   dusting*
2kg/4½lb firm fish fillet, such as
*   haddock, cod, hake or*
*   monkfish*
105ml/7 tbsp sunflower oil
30ml/2 tbsp olive oil
1 lemon, sliced
salt

For the marinade

75ml/5 tbsp olive oil
4 onions, sliced
2 unpeeled garlic cloves, slightly
*   crushed*
1 fresh rosemary sprig
1 fresh parsley sprig
about 8 sage leaves
90ml/6 tbsp white wine vinegar
sea salt

Put the flour on a plate or in a plastic bag, mix in a pinch of salt and use to dust the fish all over.

Heat the sunflower oil and olive oil in a frying pan over a low heat and sauté the fish for 4 minutes on each side. Remove with a slotted spoon and place on kitchen paper to soak up the excess oil, then arrange in a dish. Cover with slices of lemon.

To make the marinade, heat the olive oil in a small pan over a medium heat, then add the onions, garlic and herbs. Cook for 5 minutes, or until the onions are soft but not browned.

Add the vinegar, raise the heat and reduce slightly. Remove from the heat, cool completely and then pour over the fish fillets. Place in the refrigerator to marinate for 24 hours before serving.

Energy 470kcal/1956kJ; Protein 47g; Carbohydrate 7g, of which sugars 4g; Fat 28g, of which saturates 4g; Cholesterol 115mg; Calcium 43mg; Fibre 1.1g; Sodium 153mg.

COCONUT SALMON

Salmon is a robust fish and responds well to being cooked with strong flavours, as in this fragrant blend of spices, vinegar, garlic and chilli. Coconut milk adds a mellow touch.

Serves 4

4 salmon steaks, each about
   175g/6oz
1 onion, chopped
2 fresh green chillies, seeded
   and chopped
2 garlic cloves, crushed
2.5cm/1in piece fresh root
   ginger, grated
45ml/3 tbsp vegetable oil
5ml/1 tsp ground cumin
5ml/1 tsp ground coriander
175ml/6fl oz/¾ cup coconut
   milk

For the marinade

5ml/1 tsp ground cumin
10ml/2 tsp chilli powder
2.5ml/½ tsp ground turmeric
30ml/2 tbsp white wine vinegar
1.5ml/¼ tsp salt

To make the marinade, mix together 5ml/1 tsp of the ground cumin with the chilli powder, turmeric, vinegar and salt. Rub the paste over the salmon and marinate for 15 minutes.

Fry the onion, chillies, garlic and ginger in the oil for 5 minutes. Put into a food processor and process to a smooth paste.

Return the onion paste to the casserole dish. Add 5ml/1 tsp cumin, the coriander and coconut milk. Bring to the boil and simmer for 5 minutes. Add the salmon steaks, cover and cook for 15 minutes, until tender. Serve with rice.

Energy 416kcal/1729kJ; Protein 36.2g; Carbohydrate 5.2g, of which sugars 4.8g; Fat 27.9g, of which saturates 4.4g; Cholesterol 88mg; Calcium 75mg; Fibre 1.1g; Sodium 132mg.

WARM DUCK SALAD WITH POACHED EGGS

This salad looks spectacular and tastes divine, and makes a perfect light lunch or supper dish accompanied by crusty bread. The duck is marinated in a soy sauce and vinegar mixture.

Serves 4

3 skinless, boneless duck
   breasts, thinly sliced
30ml/2 tbsp soy sauce
30ml/2 tbsp balsamic vinegar
30ml/2 tbsp groundnut
   (peanut) oil
25g/1oz/2 tbsp unsalted butter
1 shallot, finely chopped
115g/4oz/1½ cups chanterelle
   mushrooms
4 eggs
50g/2oz mixed salad leaves
salt and ground black pepper
30ml/2 tbsp extra virgin olive
   oil, to serve
12 bamboo skewers, to serve

Toss the duck in the soy sauce and balsamic vinegar. Cover and chill for 30 minutes to allow the duck to infuse in the mixture.

Meanwhile, soak 12 bamboo skewers (about 13cm/5in long) in water to prevent them from burning during cooking. Preheat the grill (broiler) to medium.

Thread the duck on to the skewers, pleating them neatly. Place on a grill pan and drizzle with half the oil.

Grill (broil) for about 5 minutes, then turn the skewers and drizzle with the remaining oil. Grill for a further 3 minutes, or until the duck is cooked through and golden.

Meanwhile, melt the butter in a frying pan and cook the finely chopped shallot until softened. Add the chanterelle mushrooms and cook over a high heat for 5 minutes, stirring occasionally.

Poach the eggs while the chanterelles are cooking. Half fill a frying pan with water, add salt and heat until simmering. Break the eggs one at a time into a cup before tipping carefully into the water. Poach the eggs gently for 3 minutes, or until the whites are set. Use a draining spoon to transfer the eggs to a warm plate and trim off any untidy white edges.

Arrange the salad leaves on serving plates, then add the chanterelles and duck.

Carefully add the poached eggs. Drizzle with olive oil and season with ground black pepper.

Energy 271kcal/1132kJ; Protein 29.2g; Carbohydrate 1.5g, of which sugars 1.1g; Fat 18.6g, of which saturates 3.9g; Cholesterol 314mg; Calcium 51mg; Fibre 0.7g; Sodium 196mg.

CHICKEN AND PORK COOKED IN VINEGAR AND GINGER

This Filipino dish can also be prepared with fish, shellfish and vegetables. Use coconut vinegar for an authentic flavour, or white wine vinegar if it is unavailable.

Serves 4–6

30ml/2 tbsp coconut oil
6–8 garlic cloves, crushed whole
50g/2oz fresh root ginger, sliced into matchsticks
6 spring onions (scallions), cut into 2.5cm/1in pieces
5–10ml/1–2 tsp whole black peppercorns, crushed
30ml/2 tbsp palm sugar (jaggery) or muscovado sugar
8–10 chicken thighs, or thighs and drumsticks
350g/12 oz pork fillet (tenderloin), cut into chunks
150ml/¼ pint/⅔ cup coconut vinegar
150ml/¼ pint/⅔ cup dark soy sauce
300ml/½ pint/1¼ cups chicken stock
2–3 bay leaves
salt
stir-fried greens and cooked rice, to serve

Heat the oil in a wok, stir in the garlic and ginger and fry until fragrant and beginning to colour. Add the spring onions and black pepper and stir in the sugar.

Add the chicken and pork pieces to the wok and fry until they begin to colour.

Pour in the coconut vinegar, soy sauce and chicken stock and add the bay leaves.

Bring to the boil, reduce the heat, and cover. Simmer gently for 1 hour, until the meat is tender and the liquid has reduced.

Season the stew with salt to taste and serve with stir-fried greens and rice, over which the cooking liquid is spooned.

Energy 270kcal/1135kJ; Protein 42.2g; Carbohydrate 9g, of which sugars 7.6g; Fat 7.4g, of which saturates 1.6g; Cholesterol 118mg; Calcium 24mg; Fibre 0.6g; Sodium 1892mg.

SICHUAN CHICKEN IN KUNG PO SAUCE

Kung po sauce is a blend of beans, vinegar, rice wine, garlic and hoisin sauce that together create a starchy and syrup brown sauce to marinate poultry, vegetables and rice.

Serves 3

1 egg white
10ml/2 tsp cornflour (cornstarch)
2.5ml/½ tsp salt
2 chicken breasts, cut into small pieces
10ml/2 tbsp yellow salted beans
15ml/1 tbsp hoisin sauce
5ml/1 tsp light brown sugar
15ml/1 tbsp rice wine
15ml/1 tbsp white wine vinegar
4 garlic cloves, crushed
150ml/¼ pint/⅔ cup chicken stock
45ml/3 tbsp groundnut (peanut) oil
1 green (bell) pepper, chopped
2–3 dried chillies, broken into small pieces
115g/4oz roasted cashew nuts

Whisk the egg white, add the cornflour and salt, then stir in the chicken.

In a bowl, mash the beans. Stir in the hoisin sauce, sugar, rice wine, vinegar, garlic and stock.

In a wok, fry the chicken in the oil for 2 minutes, then drain over a bowl to collect the oil. Fry the pepper and chilli pieces in the reserved oil for 1 minute. Return the chicken to the wok with the bean sauce mixture. Bring to the boil, stir in the cashew nuts and serve garnished with coriander.

Energy 490kcal/2040kJ; Protein 37.7g; Carbohydrate 12.4g, of which sugars 2.6g; Fat 31.9g, of which saturates 5.6g; Cholesterol 82mg; Calcium 24mg; Fibre 1.9g; Sodium 204mg.

LAMB STEAKS WITH REDCURRANT VINEGAR GLAZE

This classic, simple dish is an excellent, quick recipe for cooking on the barbecue. The tangy flavour of redcurrants and red wine vinegar is a traditional accompaniment to lamb.

Serves 4

4 large fresh rosemary sprigs
4 lamb leg steaks
75ml/5 tbsp redcurrant jelly
30ml/2 tbsp red wine vinegar
salt and ground black pepper

Reserve the tips of the rosemary and chop the remaining leaves. Rub the chopped rosemary, salt and pepper all over the lamb.

Preheat the grill (broiler). Heat the redcurrant jelly gently in a small pan with 30ml/2 tbsp water. Stir in the vinegar.

Place the steaks on a foil-lined grill (broiler) rack and brush with a little of the redcurrant glaze. Cook for 5 minutes on each side, until deep golden, brushing with more glaze.

Transfer the lamb to warmed plates. Tip any juices from the foil into the remaining glaze and heat through. Pour over the lamb and serve, garnished with the reserved rosemary.

Energy 301kcal/1,258kJ; Protein 24g; Carbohydrate 12g, of which sugars 12g; Fat 17g, of which saturates 8g; Cholesterol 94mg; Calcium 10mg; Fibre 0.0g; Sodium 100mg.

STEAK WITH WARM TOMATO SALSA

A refreshing, tangy salsa of tomatoes, spring onions and balsamic vinegar makes a colourful topping for chunky, pan-fried steaks. Serve with potato wedges and a mixed leaf salad.

Serves 4

2 steaks, about 2cm/¾in thick
4 large plum tomatoes
2 spring onions (scallions)
30ml/2 tbsp balsamic vinegar
salt and ground black pepper

Trim any excess fat from the steaks, then season on both sides with salt and pepper.

Heat a non-stick frying pan and cook the steaks for 3 minutes on each side for medium rare, or longer if you prefer.

Meanwhile, put the tomatoes in a heatproof bowl, cover with boiling water and leave for 1–2 minutes, until the skins start to split.

Drain and peel the tomatoes, then halve them and scoop out the seeds. Dice the tomato flesh. Thinly slice the spring onions.

Transfer the steaks to plates and keep warm.

Add the vegetables, balsamic vinegar, 30ml/2 tbsp water and a little seasoning to the cooking juices in the pan and stir briefly until warm, scraping up any meat residue. Spoon the salsa over the steaks to serve.

Energy 291kcal/1215kJ; Protein 35.3g; Carbohydrate 5g, of which sugars 5g; Fat 14.5g, of which saturates 5.9g; Cholesterol 87mg; Calcium 22mg; Fibre 1.7g; Sodium 110mg.

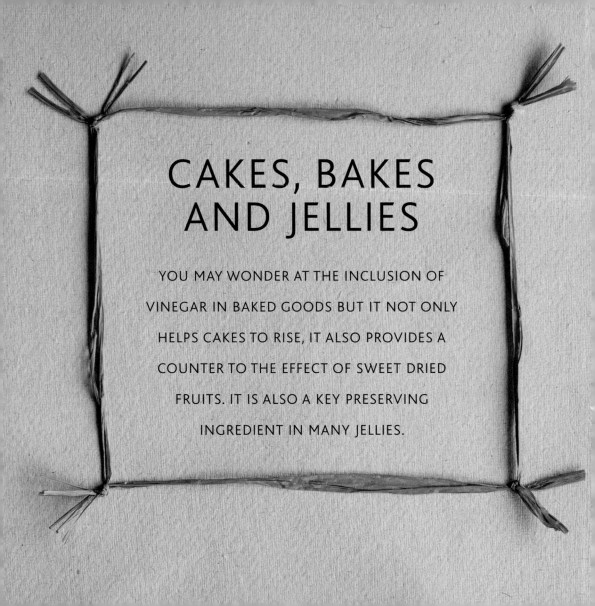

CAKES, BAKES AND JELLIES

YOU MAY WONDER AT THE INCLUSION OF

VINEGAR IN BAKED GOODS BUT IT NOT ONLY

HELPS CAKES TO RISE, IT ALSO PROVIDES A

COUNTER TO THE EFFECT OF SWEET DRIED

FRUITS. IT IS ALSO A KEY PRESERVING

INGREDIENT IN MANY JELLIES.

PAVLOVA

The main elements that make pavlova different from other meringues are the addition of cornflour and vinegar; folding in, rather than whisking in, the sugar; and the depth of the cooked meringue.

Serves 4–6
4 egg whites
225g/8oz. 1 cup sugar
15–30ml/1–2 tbsp cornflour
*   (cornstarch)*
15ml/1 tbsp white wine vinegar
300ml/½ pint/1½ cups
*   whipped cream*
450g/1lb/4 cups mixed berries

Whisk the egg whites to form soft peaks. Whisk in most of the sugar, reserving a small amount. Sift the cornflour over the meringue, then fold in the remaining sugar.

Fold in the vinegar with a large metal spoon until blended. Work gently to avoid knocking the air from the meringue.

Preheat the oven to 140°C/275°F/Gas 1. Prepare a baking sheet, drawing a 23cm/9in circle in heavy pencil on the reverse of the paper.

Spread half the mixture into a thick, flat neat round, then spoon the rest in high swirls around the edge to create a border. Bake for 1–1½ hours until the meringue is firm, checking frequently.

When cooked and cooled, peel off the paper and fill the pavlova shell with the whipped cream and the berries.

Energy 565kcal/2368kJ; Protein 5.6g; Carbohydrate 73.5g, of which sugars 66.6g; Fat 29.7g, of which saturates 18.5g; Cholesterol 78.8mg; Calcium 96.5mg; Fibre 1.3g; Sodium 104.8mg.

VINEGAR CAKE

This fruit cake is sweet and moist, and not in the least sour from the white wine vinegar. It is made using an old-fashioned recipe, which contains no eggs, and the vinegar helps the mixture to rise.

Serves 12

150g/5oz/10 tbsp butter or block margarine, diced, plus extra for greasing
300g/11oz/2⅔ cups plain (all-purpose) flour
150g/5oz/generous ½ cup soft dark brown sugar
75g/3oz/generous ¾ cup raisins
75g/3oz/¾ cup sultanas (golden raisins)
50g/2oz/⅓ cup chopped mixed (candied) peel
2.5ml/½ tsp bicarbonate of soda (baking soda)
250ml/8fl oz/1 cup milk
25ml/1½ tbsp white wine vinegar

Energy 276kcal/1159kJ; Protein 3.6g; Carbohydrate 43.4g, of which sugars 24.3g; Fat 11g, of which saturates 7g; Cholesterol 30mg; Calcium 78mg; Fibre 1.1g; Sodium 110mg.

Preheat the oven to 180°C/350°F/Gas 4. Grease and line a 20cm/8in round deep cake tin or pan.

Sift the flour into a large bowl. Add the butter and rub in until the mixture resembles fine breadcrumbs. Add the sugar and dried fruits, and stir together.

Dissolve the bicarbonate of soda in 75ml/5 tbsp of the milk and add to the dry ingredients.

Stir the vinegar into the remaining milk and pour into the bowl. Beat with a wooden spoon until smooth, then spoon into the prepared tin and smooth the top level. Indent the centre slightly.

Bake for 1 hour, then reduce the heat to 160°C/325°F/Gas 3 and bake for a further 20 minutes, or until a warmed skewer inserted into the centre comes out clean.

Cool in the tin for 5 minutes, then turn out to go cold on a wire rack. It will keep in an airtight container for 1 week.

CURRANT AND WALNUT TART

Adding a little white wine vinegar to this tart counters the sweetness of the dried currants. It is delicious served hot or cold with cream on the side.

Serves 4

For the sweet pastry

115g/4 oz/1 cup plain (all-purpose) flour

50g/2 oz/¼ cup cool unsalted butter, diced

25g/1 oz/1 tbsp icing (confectioners') sugar, sifted

1 egg yolk

For the filling

1 egg

75g/3oz/scant ½ cup soft light brown sugar

50g/2oz/¼ cup unsalted butter, melted

10ml/2 tsp white wine vinegar

115g/4oz/½ cup currants

25g/1oz/¼ cup chopped walnuts

double (heavy) cream, to serve (optional)

To make the sweet pastry, sift the flour into a mixing bowl, add the butter and rub in with your fingertips until the mixture resembles fine breadcrumbs. Stir in the sugar.

Lightly beat the egg yolk with 15ml/1 tbsp cold water. Add to the flour mixture and mix in with a round-bladed knife. Gather together to make a soft dough.

Wrap in cling film (plastic wrap) and chill for at least 30 minutes before rolling out.

To make the tart, on a lightly floured surface, roll out the sweet pastry and line a 20cm/8in flan tin or tart pan. Preheat the oven to 190°C/ 375°F/Gas 5.

Mix the egg, sugar and melted butter together. Stir the vinegar, currants and walnuts into the mixture.

Pour the mixture into the pastry case and bake for 30 minutes. Remove from the oven when thoroughly cooked, take out of the flan tin and leave to cool on a wire rack for at least 30 minutes.

Serve the tart on its own or with a dollop of fresh cream, if using.

Energy 312kcal/1,307kJ; Protein 3.4g; Carbohydrate 41.1g, of which sugars 41g; Fat 16.1g, of which saturates 7.3g; Cholesterol 74mg; Calcium 54mg; Fibre 0.8g; Sodium 99mg.

RED PEPPER AND CHILLI JELLY

The hint of chilli in this jelly makes it ideal for spicing up sausages or burgers. Use within one year and once opened, keep in the refrigerator and use within two months.

Makes about 900g/2lb

*8 red (bell) peppers, quartered
    and seeded
4 fresh red chillies, halved and
    seeded
1 onion, roughly chopped
2 garlic cloves, roughly chopped
250ml/8fl oz/1 cup water
250ml/8fl oz/1 cup white wine
    vinegar
7.5ml/1½ tsp salt
450g/1lb/2¼ cups preserving
    sugar, warmed
25ml/1½ tbsp powdered pectin*

Arrange the quartered red peppers, skin side up, on a rack in a grill (broiling) pan and grill (broil) until the skins blacken and blister.

Put the peppers in a plastic bag to steam for about 10 minutes, then carefully remove the skins.

Put the peppers, chillies, onion, garlic and water in a food processor and process to a purée. Press through a sieve or strainer set over a bowl, pressing with a spoon to extract as much juice as possible. There should be about 750ml/1¼ pints/3 cups.

Scrape the purée into a large pan, then stir in the vinegar and salt. Combine the warmed sugar and pectin, then stir it into the puréed pepper mixture. Heat gently, stirring, until the sugar and pectin have dissolved, then bring to the boil.

Cook the jelly, stirring, for 4 minutes, then remove the pan from the heat. Pour into warmed, sterilized jars. Leave to cool and set, then cover, label and store in a cool dark place.

Energy 2275kcal/9665kJ; Protein 18g;
Carbohydrate 571g, of which sugars
565.1g; Fat 6.1g, of which saturates 1.5g;
Cholesterol 0mg; Calcium 373mg; Fibre
24.8g; Sodium 89mg.

PLUM AND APPLE JELLY

Serve this rich jelly with roast meats or take to a picnic and enjoy with cold meats and crusty bread.

Makes about 1.3kg/3lb

900g/2lb plums, stoned (pitted) and chopped
450g/1lb tart cooking apples, chopped
150ml/1¼ pint/²⁄₃ cup cider vinegar
750ml/1¼ pints/3 cups water
675g/1½lb/scant 3½ cups preserving sugar

In a pan, bring the fruit, vinegar and water to the boil, reduce the heat, cover and simmer for 30 minutes. Pour into a sterilized jelly bag suspended over a bowl.

Drain for 3 hours. Measure the juice into a pan, adding 450g/1lb/2¼ cups sugar for every 600ml/1 pint/2½ cups juice. Bring to the boil, stirring, until the sugar dissolves. Boil for 10 minutes, or to setting point (105°C/220°F). Remove from heat and skim off scum. Pour into warmed sterilized jars. Cover and seal.

Store in a cool, dark place and use within 2 years. Once opened, keep refrigerated and use within 2 months.

Energy 2803kcal/11,963kJ; Protein 5.5g; Carbohydrate 740.7g, of which sugars 740.7g; Fat 0.4g, of which saturates 0g; Cholesterol 0mg; Calcium 401mg; Fibre 6.4g; Sodium 49mg.

MINTED GOOSEBERRY JELLY

This classic, tart jelly takes on a pinkish tinge during cooking, not green as one would expect.

Makes about 1.2kg/2½lb

1.3kg/3lb/12 cups gooseberries
1 bunch fresh mint
750ml/1¼ pints/3 cups cold water
400ml/14fl oz/1 ²⁄₃ cups white wine vinegar
about 900g/2lb/4½ cups preserving sugar
45ml/3 tbsp chopped fresh mint

Place the gooseberries, bunch of mint and water in a preserving pan. Bring to the boil, reduce the heat, cover and simmer for 30 minutes. Add the vinegar and simmer, uncovered, for a further 10 minutes.

Pour the fruit and juices into a sterilized jelly bag suspended over a bowl. Leave to drain for at least 3 hours, until the juices stop dripping, then measure the strained juices back into the cleaned preserving pan.

Add 450g/1lb/2¼ cups sugar for every 600ml/1 pint/2½ cups juice. Heat gently, stirring, until dissolved. Bring to the boil and cook for 15 minutes to setting point (105°C/220°F). Remove from heat and skim off scum. Cool, add the chopped mint, pour into sterilized jars, cover and seal. Use within 1 year. Once opened, keep chilled. Use within 3 months.

Energy 3641kcal/15,534kJ; Protein 10g; Carbohydrate 955.5g, of which sugars 955.5g; Fat 2g, of which saturates 0g; Cholesterol 0mg; Calcium 617mg; Fibre 12g; Sodium 64mg.

INDEX

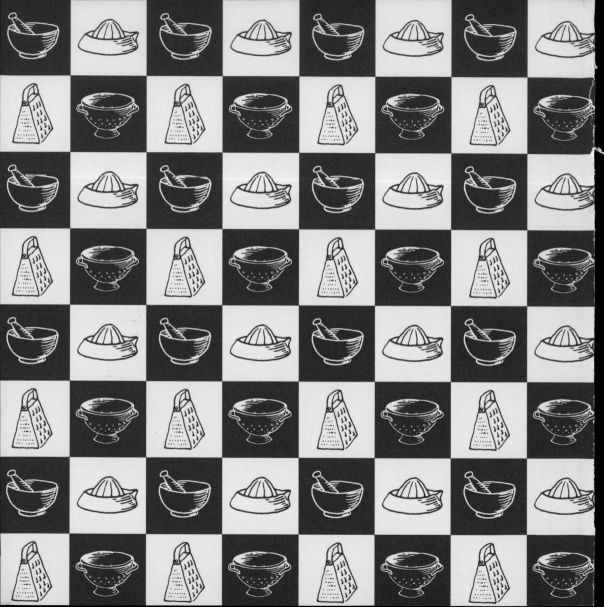